AMAZING STRUCTURES
STADIUMS

by Rebecca Pettiford

Ideas for Parents and Teachers

Pogo Books let children practice reading informational text while introducing them to nonfiction features such as headings, labels, sidebars, maps, and diagrams, as well as a table of contents, glossary, and index.

Carefully leveled text with a strong photo match offers early fluent readers the support they need to succeed.

Before Reading

- "Walk" through the book and point out the various nonfiction features. Ask the student what purpose each feature serves.
- Look at the glossary together. Read and discuss the words.

Read the Book

- Have the child read the book independently.
- Invite him or her to list questions that arise from reading.

After Reading

- Discuss the child's questions. Talk about how he or she might find answers to those questions.
- Prompt the child to think more. Ask: Have you ever been to a stadium? What did you see there?

Pogo Books are published by Jump!
5357 Penn Avenue South
Minneapolis, MN 55419
www.jumplibrary.com

Library of Congress Cataloging-in-Publication Data

Pettiford, Rebecca, author.
  Stadiums / by Rebecca Pettiford.
    pages cm. – (Amazing structures)
  Audience: Ages 7-9.
  Includes bibliographical references and index.
  ISBN 978-1-62031-214-8 (hardcover: alk. paper) –
  ISBN 978-1-62496-301-8 (ebook)
  1. Stadiums—Juvenile literature. I. Title.
  NA6860.P48 2015
  725.827—dc23

                              2014042536

Series Editor: Jenny Fretland VanVoorst
Series Designer: Anna Peterson
Photo Researcher: Anna Peterson

Photo Credits: American Spirit/Shutterstock.com; Ffooter/Shutterstock.com; Getty, 5, 20-21; jejim/Shutterstock.com; Shutterstock, 3, 8, 10-11, 23; SuperStock, 9, 16-17; Thinkstock, Cover, 6-7, 18-19; Tomasz Biderman/Shutterstock.com; Wayne Kryduba/Minnesota Twins, 12-13.

Printed in the United States of America at Corporate Graphics in North Mankato, Minnesota.

To Jared Peterson, Rachel Zalaznik, Dave Grohl, and Billy Joel–AP

TABLE OF CONTENTS

CHAPTER 1

· ·

WHAT IS A STADIUM?

Have you ever been to a football or baseball game? If you said yes, then you have been to a **stadium**.

A stadium is a structure that surrounds a **field**. You can see many outdoor sports in a stadium. You can also see concerts.

Stadiums have a long history.

The Colosseum in Rome, Italy, was built in 80 C.E. It was made of stone. It could seat more than 45,000 people. The Romans used it for **gladiator** fights.

Today, stadiums are made of concrete and steel. Some can seat more than 100,000 people.

CHAPTER 2

· ·

BUILDING STADIUMS

Before building, there are decisions to be made. What sports will be played there? Will the field be grass or **artificial turf**?

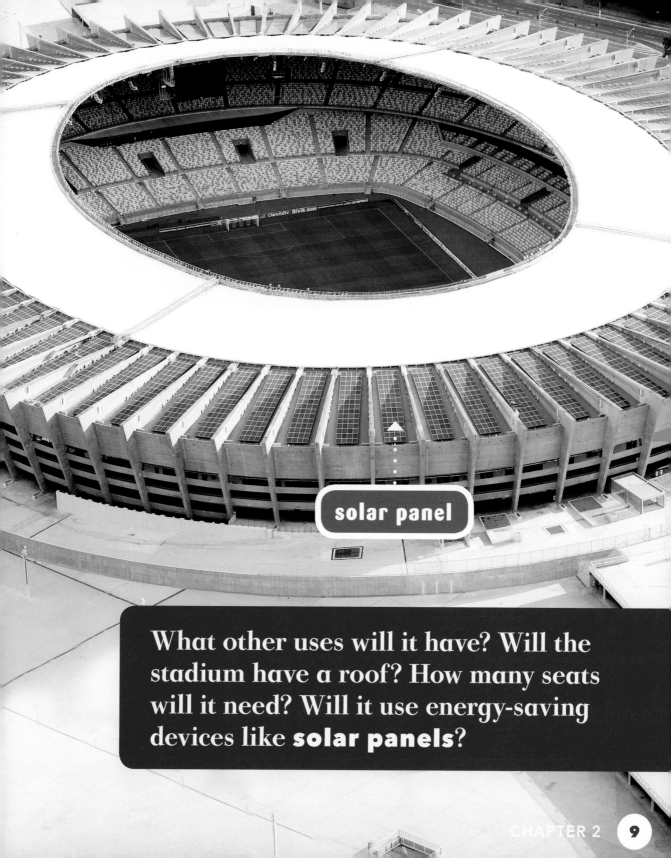

solar panel

What other uses will it have? Will the stadium have a roof? How many seats will it need? Will it use energy-saving devices like **solar panels**?

A stadium costs a lot of money. **Taxpayers** and **investors** pay for its construction. An **architect** designs it. **Engineers** make sure the land can support its weight. Workers use concrete and steel to build it.

A big company spends millions of dollars to name a stadium. Years later, a different company may buy the naming rights.

What does a stadium look like?

Let's go in.

sponsor

CHAPTER 3

AT THE STADIUM

Many stadiums are open air, but some have roofs.

dome

In some stadiums, the roofs are dome-shaped. A **dome** looks like the empty upper half of a sphere. Roofed stadiums can be loud.

Some stadiums have an oval shape. This shape is good for many sports. An oval stadium has seating all the way around the field.

TAKE A LOOK!

Some stadiums are designed to be loud. Loud cheering builds excitement. In these stadiums, roofs cover most of the seats. Noise bounces off the roofs and back into the crowd.

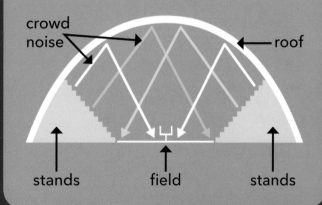

crowd noise

roof

stands

field

stands

No matter where you sit, you should have a good view of the field.

Why?

Each row of seats is a little higher than the row before it. **Aisles** make it easy for you to get to your seat. Most aisles have steps.

aisle

What are you doing this weekend?

Are you going to a game or a concert? Then you're going to a stadium.

Have fun!

ACTIVITIES & TOOLS

DRAW A STADIUM

Design and draw your own stadium!
You will need the following materials:

- drawing paper
- pencil
- eraser
- colored pencils or markers

❶ Decide what sport will be played there. What will the field look like? A football or soccer field will be rectangular. A baseball field will have a diamond shape. A running track will be oval.

❷ Draw your field on a piece of paper. Now draw a stadium around your field. Does the field's shape affect the shape you chose for the stadium?

❸ Now draw a stadium in which two different sports are played. Does the shape of the stadium change or stay the same?

❹ Use your colored pencils or markers to color the field, seats, and lights. Give your stadium a name. Have fun!

GLOSSARY

aisles: Passages between rows of seats.

architect: A person who designs stadiums and other structures.

artificial turf: A surface that looks like grass but is made from other materials.

dome: An empty upper half of a sphere.

engineers: People who plan and build stadiums and other structures.

field: A large area of land people use to play a variety of sports.

gladiator: A man from ancient Rome who was trained to fight against other men or animals.

investors: People who give money to build a stadium and expect to make more money after it's open for business.

solar panels: Panels that can absorb the sun's rays and supply energy for electricity and heat.

taxpayers: People who pay taxes, which are required by their city government.

INDEX

TO LEARN MORE

Learning more is as easy as 1, 2, 3.

1) **Go to www.factsurfer.com**

2) **Enter "stadiums" into the search box.**

3) **Click the "Surf" to see a list of websites.**

With factsurfer, finding more information is just a click away.